This Is a Let's-Read-and-Find-Out Science Book

COMETS

by Franklyn M. Branley   illustrated by Giulio Maestro

Thomas Y. Crowell   New York

HOUSTON PUBLIC LIBRARY

Other Recent Let's-Read-and-Find-Out Science Books You Will Enjoy

All Kinds of Feet · Flying Giants of Long Ago · Rain and Hail · Why I Cough, Sneeze, Shiver, Hiccup, & Yawn · You Can't Make a Move Without Your Muscles · The Sky Is Full of Stars · The Planets in Our Solar System · Digging Up Dinosaurs · No Measles, No Mumps for Me · When Birds Change Their Feathers · Birds Are Flying · A Jellyfish Is Not a Fish · Cactus in the Desert · Me and My Family Tree · Redwoods Are the Tallest Trees in the World · Shells are Skeletons · Caves · Wild and Woolly Mammoths · The March of the Lemmings · Corals · Energy from the Sun · Corn Is Maize · The Eel's Strange Journey

Let's-Read-and-Find-Out Science Books are edited by Dr. Roma Gans, Professor Emeritus of Childhood Education, Teachers College, Columbia University, and Dr. Franklyn M. Branley, Astronomer Emeritus and former Chairman of The American Museum-Hayden Planetarium. For a complete catalog of Let's-Read-and-Find-Out Science Books, write to Thomas Y. Crowell, Department 363, 10 East 53rd Street, New York, NY 10022.

Comets

Text copyright © 1984 by Franklyn M. Branley
Illustrations copyright © 1984 by Giulio Maestro

Designed by Al Cetta

Library of Congress Cataloging in Publication Data
Branley, Franklyn Mansfield, 1915-
  Comets.

  (Let's-read-and-find-out science book)
  Summary: Explains what comets are, how they are formed, and how their unusual orbits bring them into earth's view at predictable intervals, with a special focus on Halley's comet.

  1. Comets—Juvenile literature.   2. Halley's comet—Juvenile literature.   [1. Comets.   2. Halley's comet]   I. Maestro, Giulio, ill.   II. Title.   III. Series.
QB721.5.B73   1984   523.6   83-46161
ISBN 0-690-04414-3
ISBN 0-690-00415-1 (lib. bdg.)

4 5 6 7 8 9 10

Comets are parts of our solar system. Like the planets, they go around the sun.

Gas and dust tail

But comets are not made of solid rock like planets.
A comet is a ball of dust, stones and ice. Many
people call comets dirty snowballs.

The "snowball" may be only a few miles across. But when the sun heats this "snowball" much of it is changed to gases. The gases expand and form the comet's head, which may be thousands of miles across.

A comet may also have a tail, made of gases and dust. It can be millions of miles long.

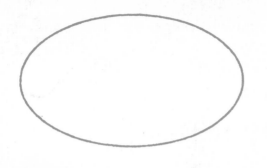

An ellipse can be flat and stretched out (like the orbit of a comet), or a nearly perfect circle (like the orbit of a planet).

Comets go around the sun. But they do not go around in circles. The path, or orbit, of a comet is a flattened circle—like the shape of a beach ball when you sit on it.

The shape of the orbit is called an ellipse. The sun is near one end of the ellipse. So during part of its journey a comet moves close to the sun. Most of the time, though, it is far away.

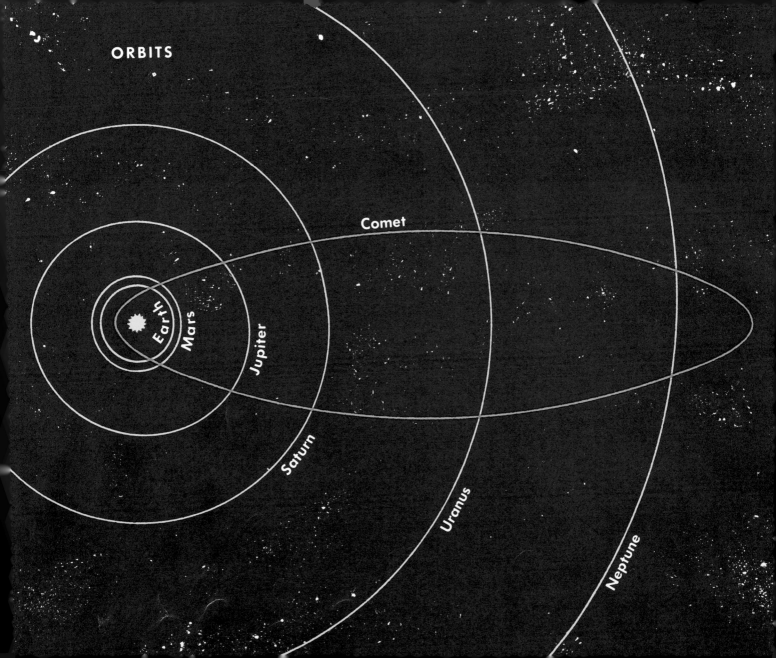

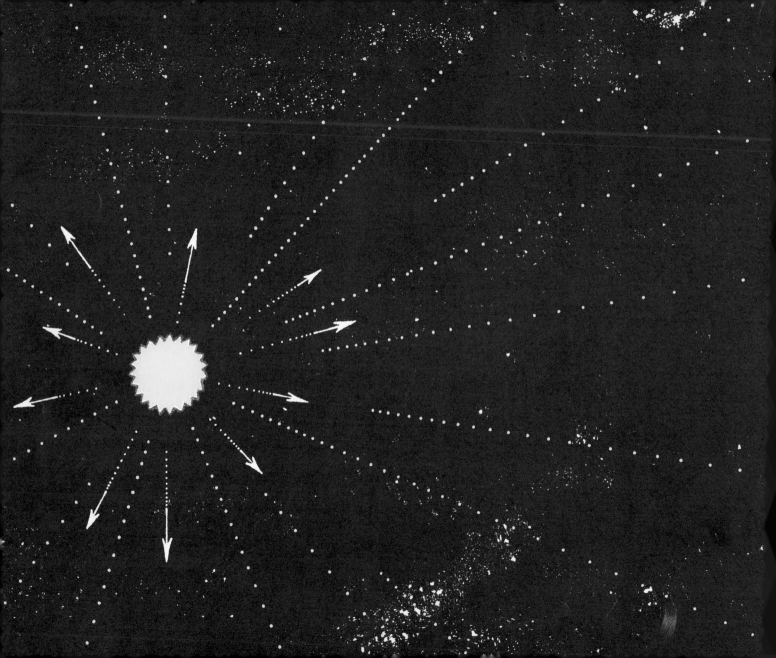

When a comet gets close to the sun, some of its dust and gases are pushed away from its head. The dust and gases stream away into space like hair. They make the comet's tail. People used to call comets "long-haired stars."

The sun gives off light—that we know. But it also throws off parts of itself—parts that are smaller than atoms. It is these particles that push the dust and gases away from the head of a comet. That's why the tail always points away from the sun.

When the comet is moving toward the sun, the tail is behind the head.

When the comet moves away from the sun, the tail
is in front of the head. But it is still called a tail.

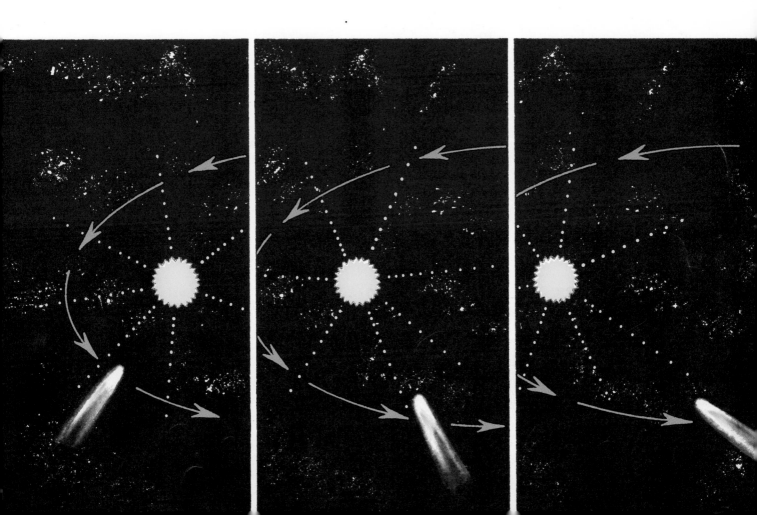

A comet moves fast in its trip around the sun. But
when we see it, the comet does not seem to move.
That's because it is so far away. The moon moves
fast, but when you look at it, you can't see any
motion. That's because the moon is far away.

So comets do not streak across the sky. You cannot see any motion. But if you look night after night, you can see that a comet changes position among the stars. If you watch the moon night after night, you'll see that it also changes position.

In January 1986 you might be able to see the most famous of all the comets. It is Halley's comet—that's HAL-ee, to rhyme with valley. You can see it because the dust in the tail reflects sunlight.

Look low in the western sky an hour or so after sunset. It will be just below the constellation Pegasus, the flying horse. Halley will be dim. You won't need a telescope to see it. But you will need to have a pair of binoculars.

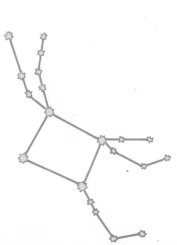

The constellation Pegasus is an upside-down flying horse. The artist "borrowed" stars from Andromeda so the horse would have back legs.

If you don't see Halley in January, you will have another chance late in March. This time look low in the sky and a bit east of south. It will be near the constellation Scorpius, the scorpion. But Halley will still be dim.

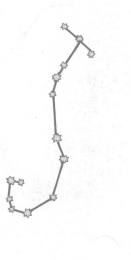

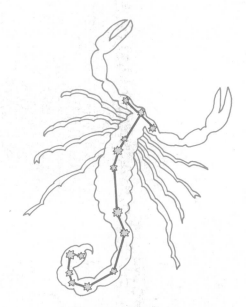

The stars in Scorpius
trace out its stinger and claws.

For maybe 3000 years, or even a lot longer, Halley has been in orbit. About every 76 years it goes around the sun and then far out beyond Jupiter before making a return trip. When Halley is close to the sun, people can see it. They see it about every 76 years.

You will see it in 1986. Julius Caesar, the Roman general, saw it in 87 B.C. when he was 13 years old.

People saw it in 1835 when Mark Twain was born. He was the man who wrote *Tom Sawyer*. The comet appeared again in 1910; that's when Mark Twain died.

Edmund Halley, an English astronomer, saw the comet in 1682. He discovered that the comet moves around the sun in an orbit shaped like an ellipse.

He also said it would return 76 years later. And it did. That's why the comet is named after him. Before Halley told them, people thought comets just wandered around the sky.

Halley lived about 300 years ago. In those days many people were afraid of comets. They thought a comet was a warning of something terrible that would soon occur. There might be a war, or a flood, or a famine. Perhaps there would be an earthquake. Others thought comets spread poison gases around the earth.

Comets were called disasters. The word "disaster" means evil star: *dis* means evil, and *aster* means star.

Comets are visitors that we see every once in a while. So they are exciting. But we know that comets cannot make terrible things happen.

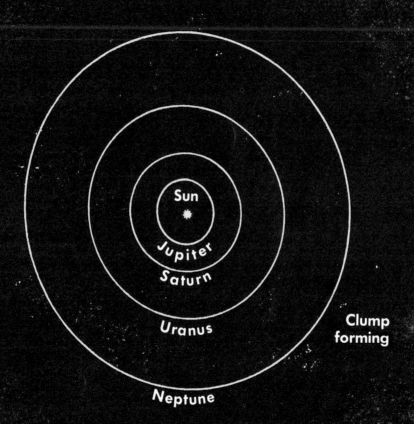

Dust and gas cloud

Sun

Jupiter

Saturn

Uranus

Clump
forming

Neptune

There are millions—maybe even billions—of comets in our solar system. New ones are probably forming all the time.

Way out beyond the sun and the planets there is a big cloud of dust and gases. It surrounds the solar system. Scientists believe that comets are formed from the dust and gases of this cloud.

No one knows exactly how comets are formed, but some scientists think it happens like this:

The particles of dust and gas are loose and far apart. All of them are moving. Once in a while, some of the particles collide and join together to make a clump. The clump collides with other particles, and so it grows larger.

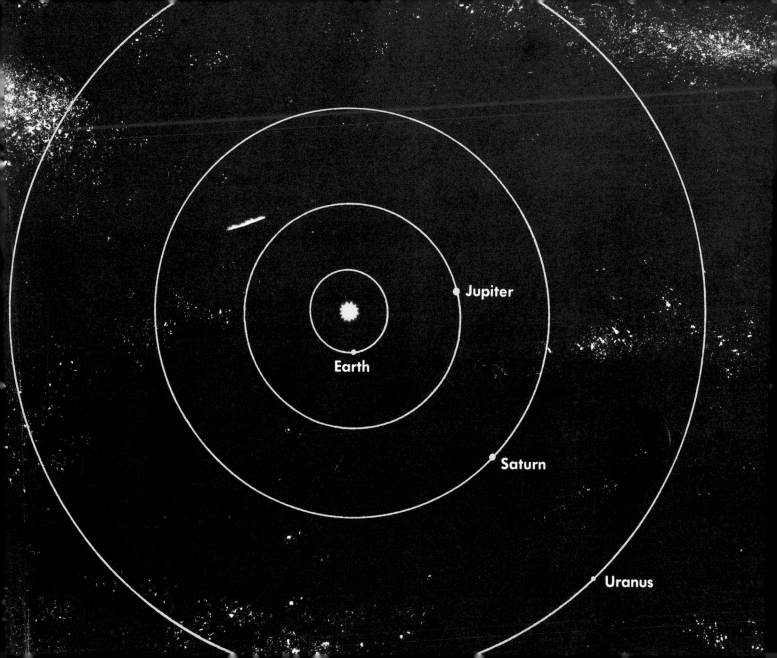

Neptune

The clump may be pulled out of the cloud by a star
as it passes by the solar system.
Its gravity pulls on the clump.
Jupiter also pulls on the clump. Jupiter is a
giant planet, and it has strong gravity.

Clump

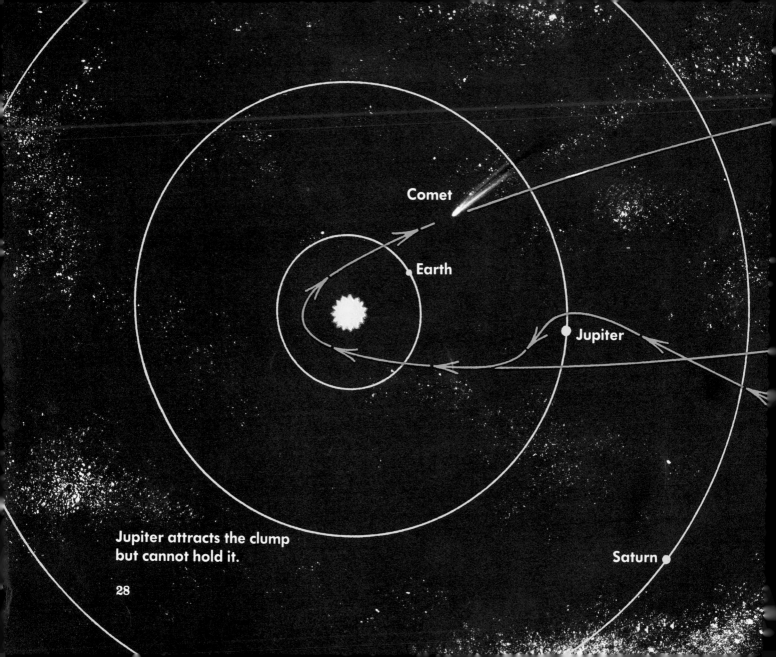

Comet

Earth

Jupiter

Saturn

Jupiter attracts the clump
but cannot hold it.

28

Neptune

Uranus

Path of comet

Path
of clump

The clump is pulled into the solar system. It goes
into orbit around the sun because of the sun's even
stronger gravity. It has become a comet.

Each year astronomers discover new comets.
Some of them are seen only once. They make one
trip around the sun and then go way out into space.
The sun's gravity cannot hold them.

29

Halley has been
losing dust for
thousands of years.
Even after Halley has
disappeared entirely its
dust will remain in the
solar system.

Other comets, like Halley, keep returning. They
have been captured by the sun. Halley's earliest visit
was probably 3000 years ago. It may keep returning
for another 3000 years.

But every time a comet goes around the sun, the comet loses part of itself. Gases and dust are pulled out of the comet. That's why Halley is now dimmer than it used to be. Next time it visits us, in 2062, it may be even dimmer. Each visit it may get dimmer and dimmer, until it finally disappears.

Look for Halley in 1986. It will be the same comet that was seen by Edmund Halley, and by Julius Caesar long before Halley saw it. And it was seen by people long before Caesar was born. Who knows, you may see Halley in 2062. You can show it to your grandchildren.

Between 1986 and 2062 you may see many other comets. Some of them will be comets we already know about. Others will be new. They will be making their first journey around the sun.